TIME SPACE AND DRUMS PART TWO

JAZZ
DRUMMING
Foundation

TIME SPACE AND DRUMS PART TWO

JAZZ DRUMMING Foundation

GRAVITY Volume 2 - Getting Grounded

The Time Space & Drums Series
A Complete Program of Lessons in Professional, Contemporary Rock, and Jazz Drumming Styles.

Written and Developed By:
Stephen Hawkins

Graphic Design By: Nathaniel Dasco.
Special Thanks To Linda Drouin and Ikhide Oshoma

ThinkeLife Publications

Time Space and Drums Copyright 2020 By Stephen Hawkins.

All Rights Reserved.

No part of this book may be reproduced in any form or by any electronic or mechanical means including information storage and retrieval means without permission in writing from the author.

The only exception is by a reviewer, who may quote short excerpts in a review.

Stephen Hawkins - Time Space and Drums
Visit my website at www.timespaceanddrums.com

First printing: August 2020.

ISBN: 978 1 913929 01 5

Dedicated to the late Paul Daniels and family, Martin Daniels, Trevor Daniels, Paul Mellor's, Keith, Peter Windle, Andrew Marple's, Colin Keys, Peters & Lee, Susan Maughan, Ronnie Dukes, Tom O'Connor, Les Dennis, Bob Monkhouse, Bobby Davro, Tommy Bruce, Robert Young, Sandie Gold as well as the hundreds of other people who have played a part in my life experience. Including Sphinx Entertainment, E & B Productions as well as the hundreds of fantastic personalities I have had the pleasure of working alongside over the past 35 years. Apologies for anyone I have missed, not forgetting the current reader who I hope will receive as much from their drumming as I have and more - Stephen Hawkins.

Table of Contents

DRUM ROLL, PLEASE! Introduction 1

NOTE VALUES 4

Lesson 1: 12/8 Jazz Beat & Drum Fills 6

Lesson 2: 4/4 Shuffle Beat & Drum Fills 13

Lesson 3: Closed Hi-Hat & Ride Cymbal Jazz Beats & Drum Fills 18

Lesson 4: Using The Brushes 23

Lesson 5: 1/16th Note Shuffle Beat 26

Lesson 6: 1/16th Drum Fills 29

RUDIMENTARY 33

Triplets 33

Disciplined Experimentation 34

Featured Drummer Recommendations 35

Buddy Rich 35

Conclusion 36

DRUM ROLL, PLEASE!

INTRODUCTION

If you recall from the Rock Drumming Foundation book, I iterated that drumming should not in any way shape or form, be a process of division. With that in mind, think of the times when you were taught to play a complex drum beat or phrase. In 99% of cases, you would have been taught to divide everything up into smaller pieces such as the bass drum pattern, then the snare drum pattern, followed by the right-hand pattern. You would then work on your left foot followed by both feet together, then add the snare drum using the left hand. By dividing everything up you eventually build the pattern up into a complete beat or phrase.

In normal circumstances, that process, or something similar, is a good idea and it is the way to get everything working together. However, there is one important distinction that you must take with you into your drumming as you develop further, thus incorporating other patterns of various complexity.

That important distinction is the way that you think about the whole process. So, if you follow most teacher's advice, you will indeed begin to divide everything which often results in success. However, instead of dividing everything up, you should instead be thinking of integrating everything. Why?

Well, if you cannot play a particular pattern, beat, or rhythm, the limbs are already divided. Your left-hand doesn't know what the right-hand is doing and so on. And so, you practice the right-hand, then practice the left-hand, then practice them both together. Then you do the same with the feat until you have brought everything together into a smooth-flowing rhythm.

The subtle difference is realizing that the limbs are already uncooperative and so, instead, shift your thinking to integration or bringing together. Play each limb one at a time until everything is brought together. As you develop over the years, you then become accustomed to a better habit of bringing things together and not dividing them. You in effect bring order to chaos as opposed to bringing chaos into order and to create order from that chaos. It's a small but significant shift in the drummer's thinking.

The point being that, as a drummer, you are on a journey to continuously create harmony and integration within yourself and your playing.

So, when it comes to the Rock Drumming Foundation and Jazz Drumming Foundation, we are really speaking of The Foundation of Drumming in general. Yes, the two styles are often separated but, in the end, and when you take a closer look, they are part of the same system or foundation. And as such, the drummer should be able to smoothly flow from one style to the other and back again in a variety of ways that further enhance each style and the flow of time that is a silent undercurrent of the drumming being played.

By this point, you should have already mastered the Rock Drumming Foundation and so congratulations are in order for making it this far. You should now have a solid foundation of rock drumming skills. However, you still have a lot ahead of you if you're a beginner. And remember, the process to develop and enhance this current jazz drumming foundation goes much the same as with the rock drumming foundation.

It is important that you master each exercise then bring everything together until the basic beats are learned. Ensure that some degree of control and flow is gained through adding the basic drum fills. Then…

1. When you can play each lesson and have spent 1 week just practicing that lesson, go through the book until you have completed each lesson over a 6-week period. Spend 1 week on each lesson.
2. Then, go through the book by spending a whole day practicing and striving for greater precision for 6 days, with 1 day per lesson. *(If you are so inclined, you can spend 24 hours on each lesson; of course, that will take more than 1 day of practicing 1 hour per day).*
3. Then, go through the whole book in 6 hours.
4. Afterwards, you should go through the book, moving from one exercise to the next, all the time striving for greater precision as you play through the whole book in a single practice session.
5. You can then begin to add technique to the equation to further improve the feel and flow of the exercises.
6. When you are at this point, you should begin your 10,000-hours practice as suggested in the Rock Drumming Foundation Course book.

But let's not get ahead of ourselves. The first, or next step after developing a rock drumming foundation is to develop a foundation of jazz rhythms, along with the basic but essential drum fills. We will then develop those drum fills in order to fuse the contents of books 1 and 2 together.

Book 2 is slightly more difficult to master, but there are only 3 rhythms to grasp. There is also a variation of the third drum rhythm.

Remember to keep revising the rhythms in book 1 on a daily basis, and also to perfect each exercise within this book as they are presented. There are no prizes for the first to finish. As always, the key to becoming proficient in jazz style rhythms is practice, practice, practice, and remember: "The stronger the foundation is, the higher the structure."

Also, take note that the time that you spend practicing should be perfect practice. This means that you should focus on what needs to be mastered rather than going off on random tangents and simply playing what comes to mind. They say that practice makes perfect but the reality is that "Perfect Practice Makes Perfect."

It would also serve you to know and understand that the contents of books 1 and 2 form the foundation of all drumming as previously suggested. Everything else in drumming is a variation or development of the contents of these first two books, so mastery of the contents of books 1 and 2 is highly advised.

Good luck and have fun.

Stephen Hawkins.

Free Audio Demonstrations

You should visit the following URL to download audio demonstrations of every exercise in this book as soon as possible. You will then receive additional tips and guidance through the included essence emails.

www.timespaceanddrums.com/tsd-2cd.html

NOTE VALUES

The majority of book 2 is written on the subject of jazz style drumming. It is, therefore, necessary to go into the notation that most jazz style drumming is based on: Triplets.

You should already know that in a bar of 4/4 music, there are 4 crotchets or what some call 1/4 notes (quarter notes); you should also know that there are 4 x 1/16th notes, and/or 8 x 1/8th notes in a bar of 4/4 music.

Let's now add another group of notes to the equation—triplets.

There are 3 triplets to each quarter note in a bar of music. That means there are 12 triplets all together in each bar. If you say out loud "One Trip-let," you will know exactly what a group of three triplets sounds like.

To count a full bar of 4/4 music in time, the click of the metronome would land on 1, 2, 3, and 4, just as it was in the first book in this series: triplets are no different.

If you count "1-Trip-let", "2-Trip-let", "3-Trip-let", "4-Trip-let", you should have no problem with the following exercises. See the diagram below to see how this looks when written.

Example 1

You could miss the second triplet in each group of three triplets out, and it would look like the diagram below. Remember the 1/8th note rest from book 1?

Example 2

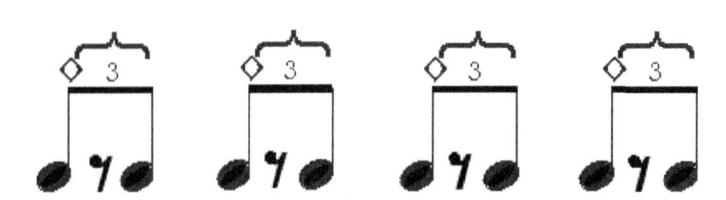

You could also miss out the second and third triplets on beats 1 and 3 to make them quarter notes and miss out the second triplet on beats 2 and 4, and then it would look like the diagram below.

Example 3

The three examples that we have just seen are the three right-hand patterns that we are going to be working on within this book. You will learn what they sound like as we go, but for now, just make sure you understand how these three patterns are formed. Re-read this section a couple of times if you would like to become familiar with the formation of these three fundamental rhythms or patterns.

Below is a diagram showing the relationship between the three jazz style patterns just mentioned, and the quarter note, (crotchet) in a bar of 4/4 music.

After studying the notation diagram, you can begin lesson 1, exercise 1.

Before moving onto lesson 1, please go to page 31 and read the Rudimentary section then return here to begin the lesson.

Lesson 1

12/8 Jazz Beat & Drum Fills.

Exercise 1

Begin by setting your metronome to a slow tempo, (60 BPM). The diamond symbol represents 1 click from the metronome. When you are ready, count 1, 2, 3, 4 continuously, until you can count evenly, and on time with the click of the metronome. Then with your right hand on the closed hi-hat cymbals proceed to play exercise 1.

Remember to think in groups of three. That is, "1-Trip-let", "2-Trip-let", "3-Trip-let" etc.

Exercise 1

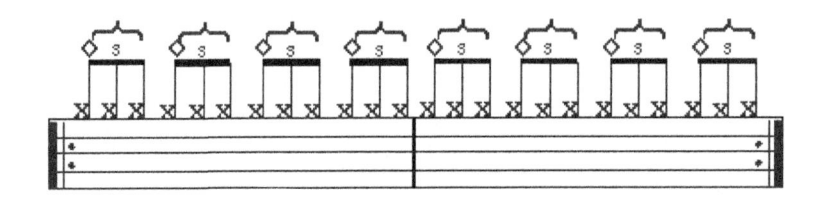

Exercise 2

When you're ready, add the bass drum on beats 1 and 3. Count along with the right hi-hat beats you played in exercise 1. It may be easier to play exercise 1 repeatedly until you can mentally see and hear where the bass drum beats go.

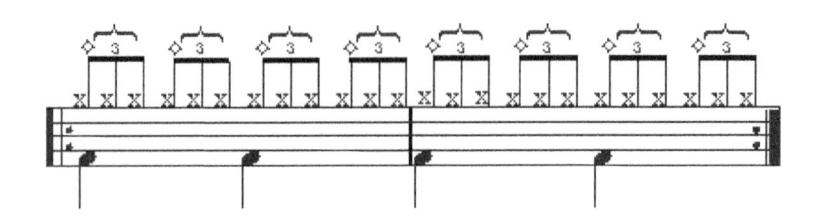

Exercise 2

Exercise 3

Now add the snare drum on beats 2 and 4. Again, play exercise 2 repeatedly until you can mentally see and hear where the snare drum beats go.

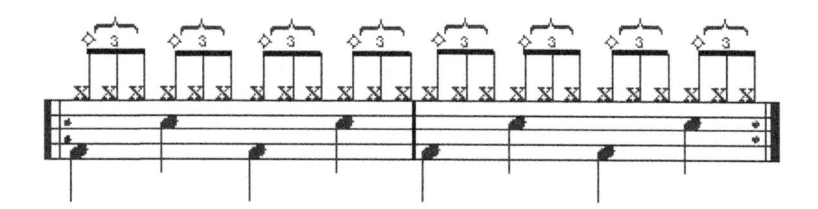

Congratulations, you've just played your first jazz style rhythm. Practice it at all volume levels and all tempos before going any further. Perfect it as much as possible.

Exercise 4

This time play the right hand over on the ride cymbal. It is the exact same rhythm as exercise 1.

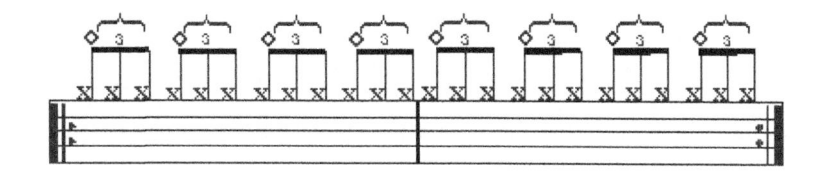

Exercise 5

Now play your right foot on the hi-hat cymbals on beats 1, 2, 3, and 4, as indicated.

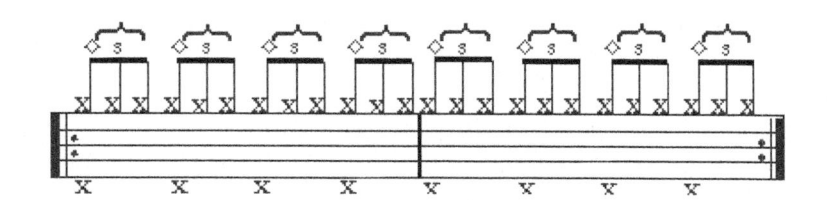

Exercise 6

Now add the bass drum on beats 1 and 3. Remember to count along with the right hi-hat beats you played in exercise 1.

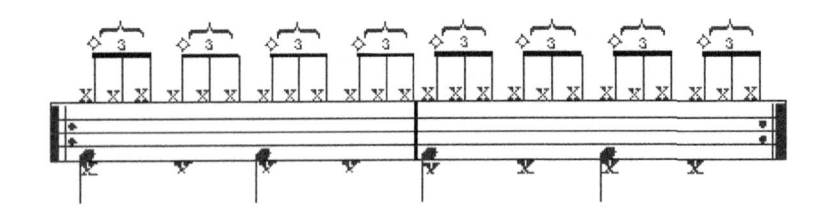

Exercise 7

Now add the snare drum on beats 2 and 4.

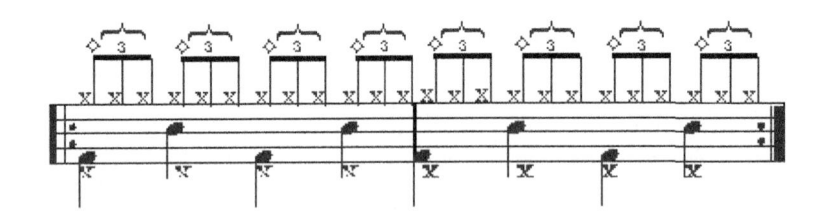

Exercise 8

Up until now, you have only played 1/4 notes and 1/4 note variations which included 1/8th notes and 1/16th notes. This means that the count has always been 1, 2, 3, 4, etc. You should now have an idea of how the triplet style pattern sounds in comparison to the rick style patterns we covered in book 1.

Now let's move on to the triplet drum fill. This will be the universal fill we use through lessons 1-4 of this book.

As mentioned in the introduction on note values, you count:

"One Trip-let", "Two Trip-let", "Three Trip-let", "Four Trip-let", and so on. The sticking has always been with your right-hand lead.

This changes when playing triplet drum fills. You will notice that beats 2 and 4 are left-hand lead sticking. The sticking in the jazz style triplet drum fills is as follows:

RLR, LRL, RLR, LRL.

Imagine counting triplets over that sticking. It is quite easy. However, because beats 2 and 4 are "LRL", sticking it can become quite awkward. You have to begin thinking on beats 1, 2, 3, and 4... R, L, R, L. This begins to convey the pulse for you. Try hitting the first note in every group of three triplets louder than the other 2, and you will have a better idea of how it should sound.

Now set your metronome and start counting triplets along with it. Count over and over again and you will begin to hear the 1, 2, 3, and 4 clearly, with the second and third triplet evenly spaced between. So, let's have a go.

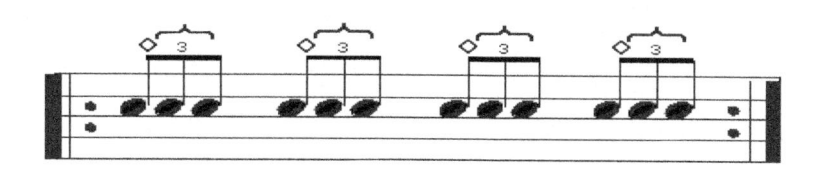

Exercise 9
This time, add the bass drum on beats 1, 2, 3, and 4. Again, you may like to try playing the bass drum for a few bars until you get used to playing 1, 2, 3, and 4 on the bass drum whilst counting and thinking triplets.

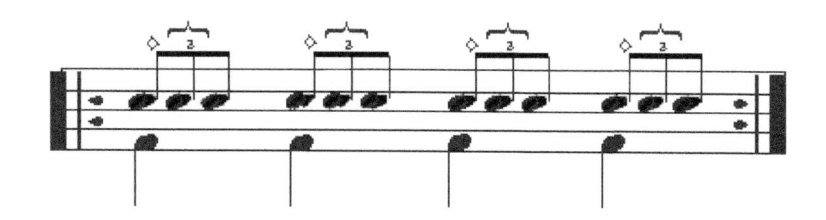

Exercise 10
Now play the same thing around the tom-toms: 3 beats on each drum, 3 on the SD, 3 on the HT, 3 on the MT, and 3 on the LT.

Because you are playing RLR, LRL, RLR, LRL, you will notice that there are 2 right-hands on the snare drum, followed by 2 left-hands on the HT, followed by 2 RH on the MT then, finally, 2 LH on the LT. This alternating means that you move up to the HT with the LH then move to the MT with the RH and finally with the LH to the LT. And of course, you will notice that your hands and arms move in a circular motion.

When you feel comfortable just playing the exercise at a very slow tempo without the metronome, you can add the metronome to begin making the drum fill flow.

Exercise 11

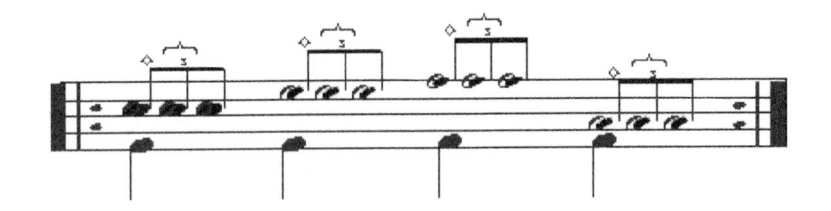

Once you are used to playing exercises 1 through 10, try the following exercise. Play 3 bars (exercise 3), then a drum fill (exercise 10) around the tom-toms. Then 3 bars (exercise 3) then a drum fill. Keep this going until you can play it continuously and smoothly before going on.

Exercise 12

Now do the same thing again, but this time try playing exercise 7 for 3 bars, then a drum fill. You should try to play the hi-hat throughout the drum fill too, along with the bass drum.

Exercise 13

Now try playing the drum fill on beats 2, 3, and 4 of the fourth bar. Make sure you understand the movements you will be making throughout the exercise. For example:

RH HH 3 bars, RH for 1 beat then: RLR, LRL, RLR,

Time Space and Drums   Gravity: Volume Two

You can see that the last note of the drum fill is played on the snare drum (or tom-tom) and is played with the RH. This means you will have to move quickly back to the HH.

But don't make it a rush. The key is to slow it down until you make the transition from drum fill to drum beat fluently.

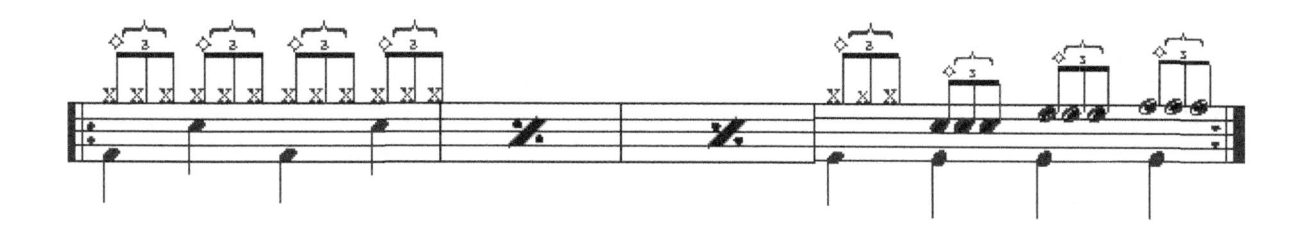

Exercise 14
Now try playing exercise 7 for 3 bars then the fill on beats 2, 3, and 4 of bar 4.

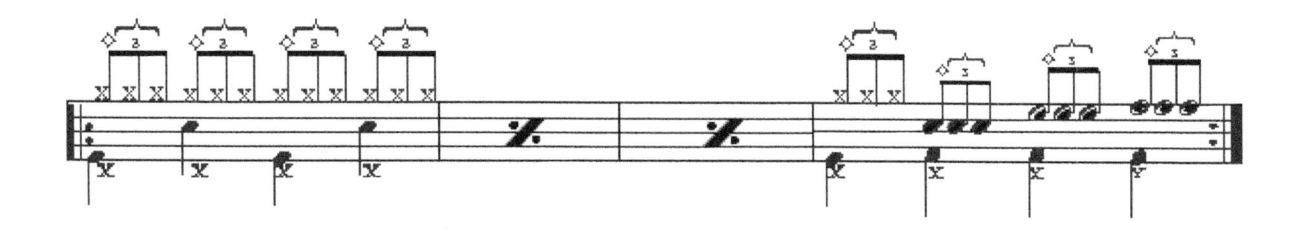

Exercise 15
Now play exercise 3 for 3 bars, then play the drum fill on beats 3 and 4 of bar 4.

Exercise 16
Now play exercise 7 for 3 bars, then play the drum fill on beats 3 and 4 of bar 4.

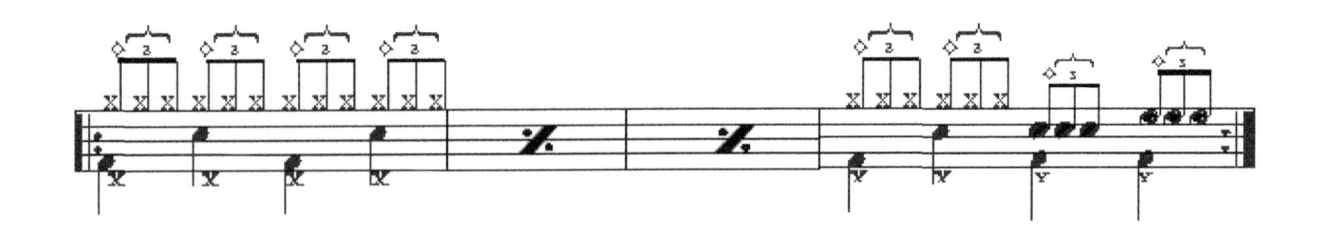

Exercise 17

This time play exercise 3 for 3 bars, then play the drum fill on beat 4 of bar 4. The fill is played on the SD only.

Exercise 18

Now play exercise 7 for 3 bars, then play the drum fill on beat 4 of bar 4.

Lesson 2

4/4 Shuffle Beat & Drum Fills

Exercise 1

Begin by setting your metronome to a slow tempo, (60 BPM). When you are ready, count 1, 2, 3, 4 until you can count evenly, and on time with the click. Then with your right-hand on the hi-hat cymbals, proceed to play exercise 1.

Try repeating exercise 1, lesson 1 but play the second of each group of triplets on a cushion. You will only hear the notes in the next exercise. This will tell you how it sounds.

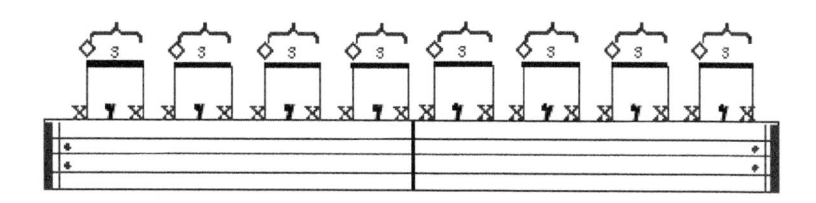

Exercise 2

Now add the bass drum on beats 1 and 3. Remember to count along with the right hi-hat beats you played in exercise 1. It may be easier to play exercise 1 repeatedly until you can mentally see and hear where the bass drum beats go.

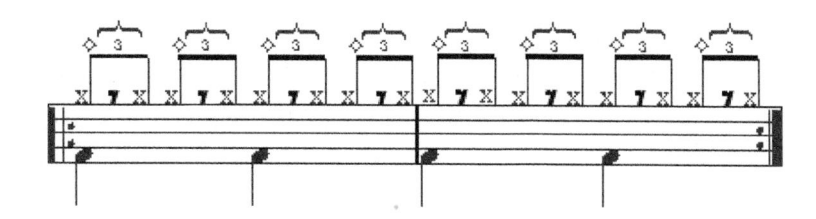

Exercise 3

Now add the snare drum on beats 2 and 4. Again, play exercise 2 repeatedly until you can mentally see and hear where the snare drum beats go.

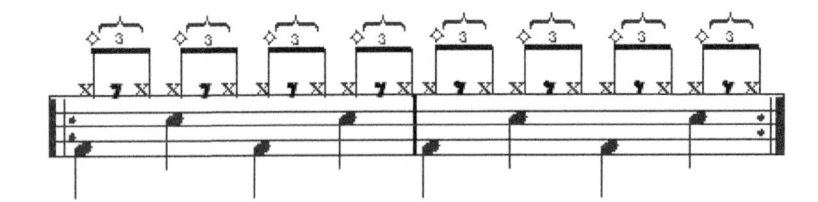

Practice exercise 3 at all volume levels and all tempos before going any further. Perfection is the aim but, of course, remember that perfection takes time.

Exercise 4
This time play the right-hand over on the ride cymbal. It is the exact same rhythm as exercise 1.

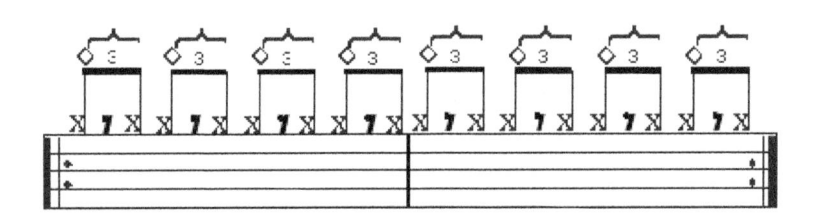

Exercise 5
Now play your right foot on the hi-hat cymbals on beats 1, 2, 3, and 4, as indicated.

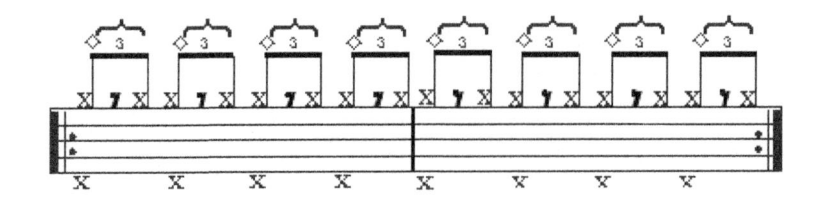

Exercise 6
Now add the bass drum on beats 1 and 3. To help you get this exercise, you might want to practice playing just your feet, to begin with.

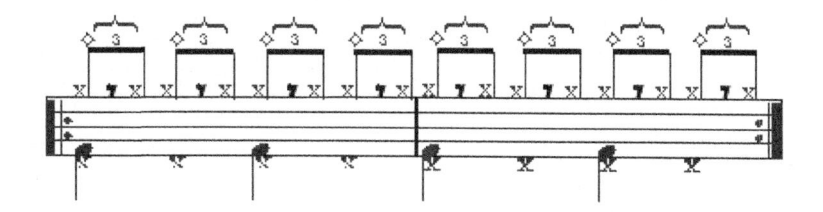

Exercise 7
Now add the snare drum on beats 2 and 4. Again, play exercise 6 repeatedly until you can mentally see and hear where the snare drum beats go.

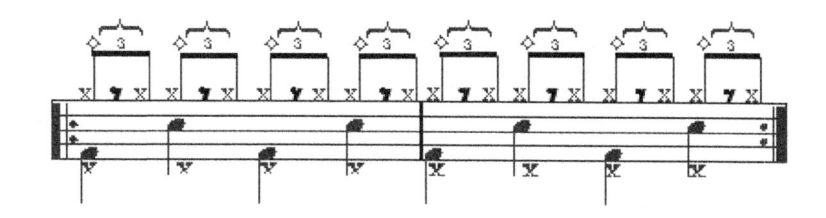

Exercise 8
Once you are used to playing exercises 1 through 7, try the following exercise. Play 3 bars (exercise 3), then a drum fill (exercise 8) around the tom-toms. Then 3 bars (exercise 3) then a drum beat. Keep this going until you can play it smoothly before going on.

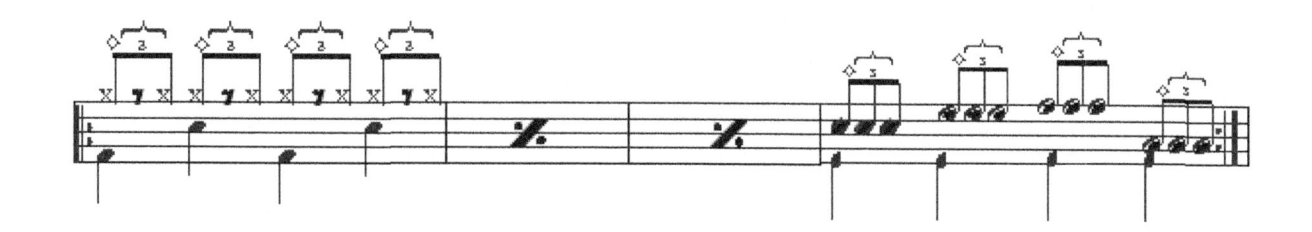

Exercise 9
Now do the same thing again, but this time try playing exercise 7 for 3 bars, then a drum fill. You should try to play the hi-hat throughout the drum fill too, along with the bass drum.

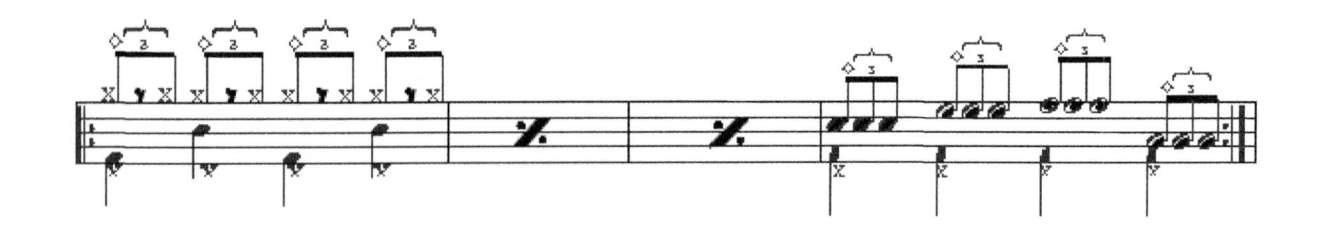

Exercise 10
Now try playing the drum fill on beats 2, 3, and 4 of the fourth bar.

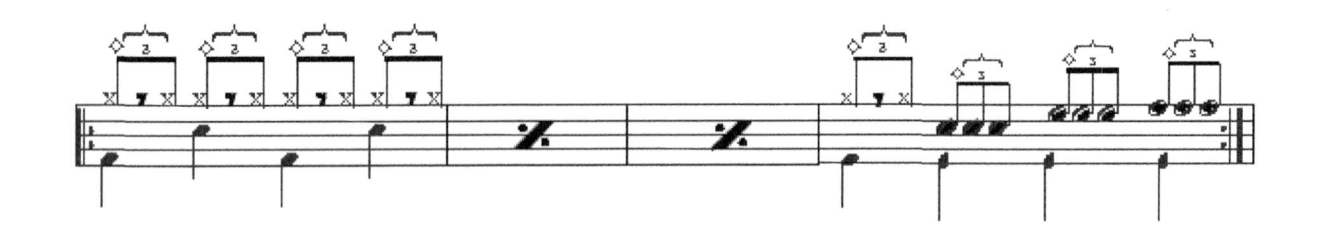

Exercise 11
Now try playing exercise 7 for 3 bars then the fill on beats 2, 3, and 4 of bar 4.

Exercise 12
Now play exercise 3 for 3 bars, then play the drum fill on beats 3 and 4 of bar 4.

Exercise 13
Now play exercise 7 for 3 bars, then play the drum fill on beats 3 and 4 of bar 4.

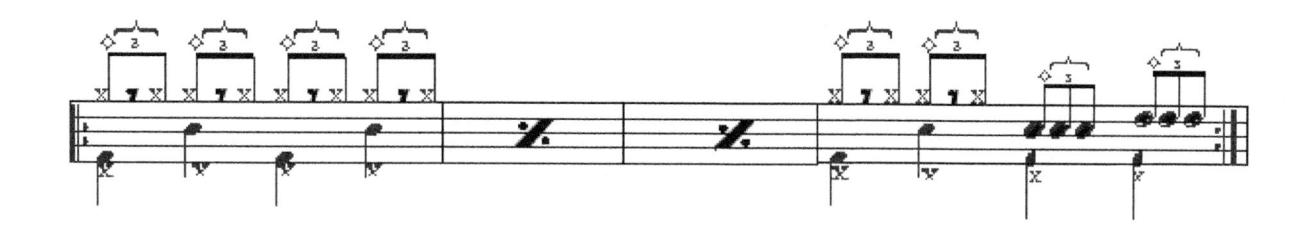

Exercise 14
This time play exercise 3 for 3 bars, then play the drum fill on beat 4 of bar 4. The fill is played on the SD only.

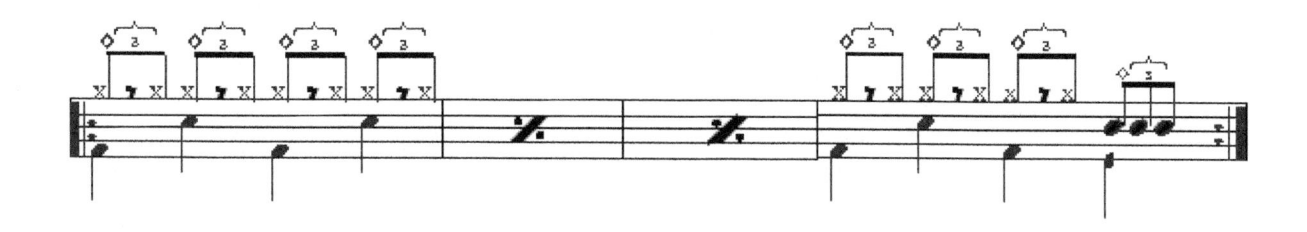

Exercise 15
Now play exercise 7 for 3 bars, then play the drum fill on beat 4 of bar 4.

Lesson 3

Closed Hi-Hat & Ride Cymbal Jazz Beats & Drum Fills

Exercise 1

Begin by setting your metronome to a slow tempo, (60 BPM). This next exercise contains, on beats 1 and 3, 1/4 notes, and on beats 2 and 4, a shuffle beat as covered in lesson 2.

You shouldn't have any problems with these exercises because they simply mix the 1/4 note and the shuffle. You now know what each sounds like, so let's have a go. The right-hand is played on the closed hi-hat as usual.

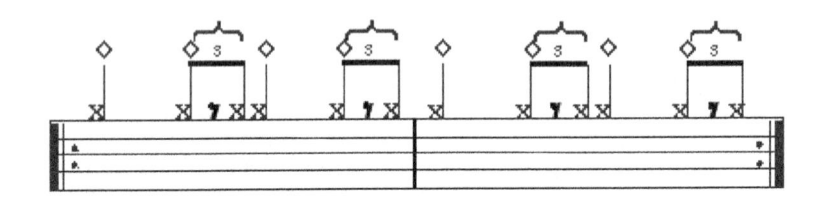

Exercise 2

Now add the bass drum on beats 1 and 3. Remember to count along with the right hi-hat beats you played in exercise 1.

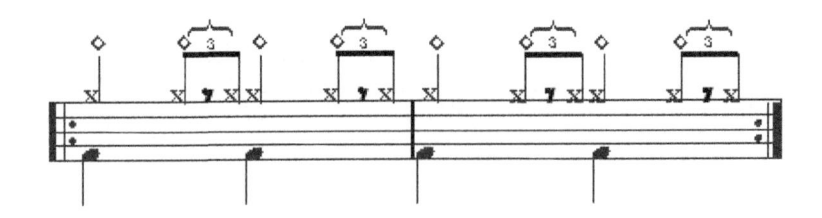

Exercise 3

Now add the snare drum on beats 2 and 4.

Time Space and Drums

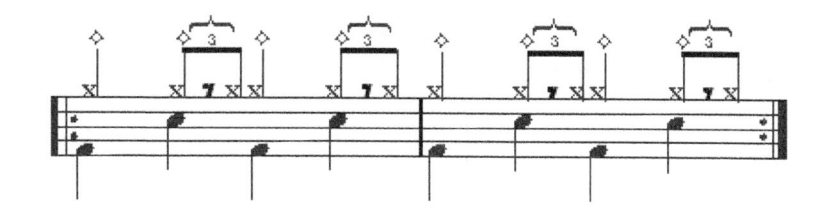

Gravity: Volume Two

Exercise 4
This time play the right-hand over on the ride cymbal. It is the exact same rhythm as exercise 1.

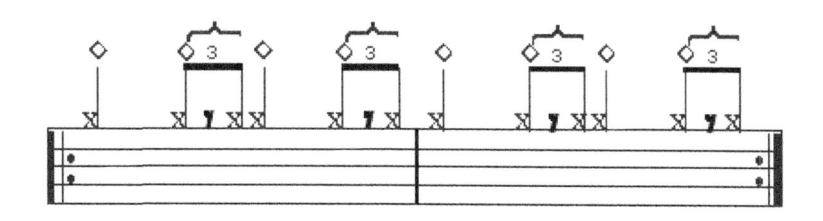

Exercise 5
Now play your right foot on the hi-hat cymbals on beats 2 and 4, as indicated.

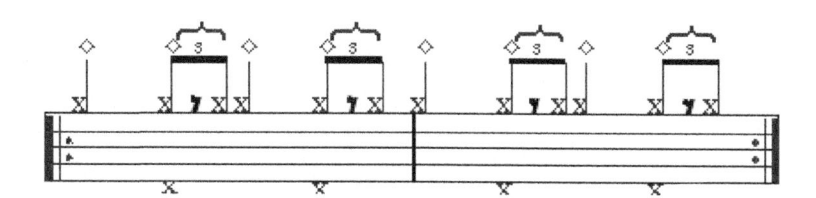

Exercise 6
Now add the bass drum on beats 1 and 3. To help you get this exercise, you might want to practice playing just your feet, to begin with. You play the BD on beat 1, the HH on beat 2, the BD on beat 3, then the HH on beat 4.

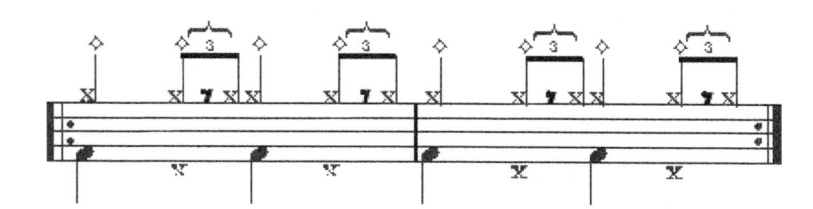

Exercise 7

Now add the snare drum on beats 2 and 4.

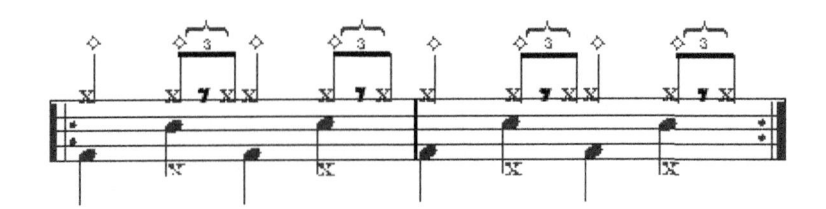

Exercise 8

This time play exercise 3 for 3 bars, then the triplet drum fill on bar 4. Remember to pay attention to the flow.

Exercise 9

Now do the same thing again, but this time try playing exercise 7 for 3 bars, then a drum fill. You should try to play the hi-hat throughout the drum fill too, along with the bass drum.

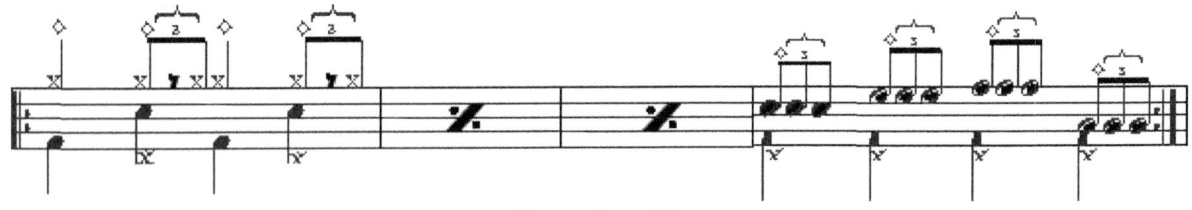

Exercise 10

Now try playing the drum fill on beats 2, 3, and 4 of the fourth bar. Play exercise 3 for 3 bars.

Time Space and Drums Gravity: Volume Two

Exercise 11
Now try playing exercise 7 for 3 bars then the fill on beats 2, 3, and 4 of bar 4.

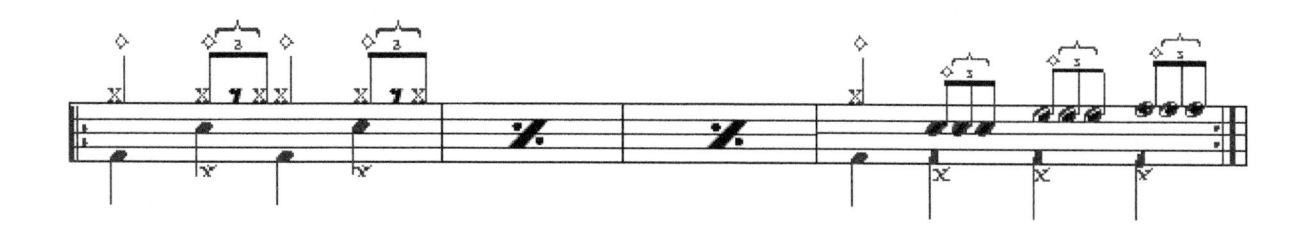

Exercise 12
Now play exercise 3 for 3 bars, then play the drum fill on beats 3 and 4 of bar 4.

Exercise 13
Now play exercise 7 for 3 bars, then play the drum fill on beats 3 and 4 of bar 4.

Exercise 14
This time play exercise 3 for 3 bars, then play the drum fill on beat 4 of bar 4. The fill is played on the SD only.

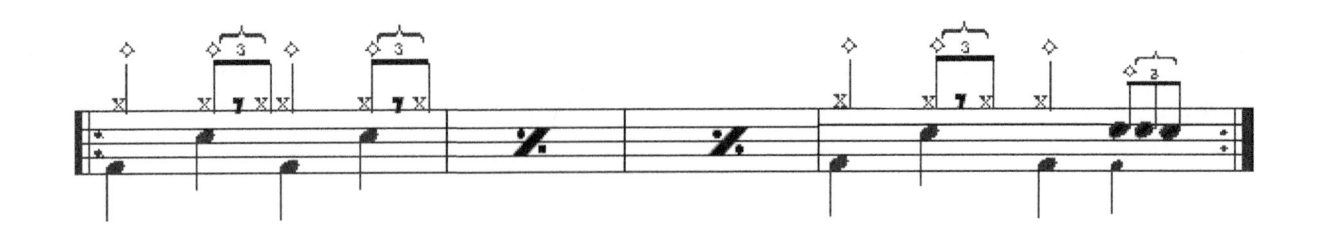

Exercise 15

Now play exercise 7 for 3 bars, then play the drum fill on beat 4 of bar 4.

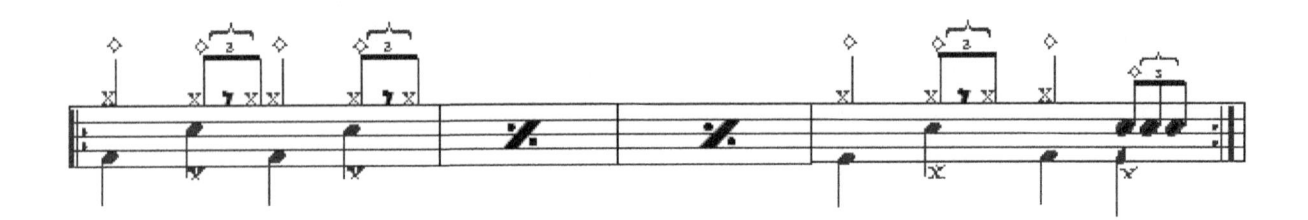

Lesson 4

Using the Brushes

As you become accustomed to playing the drums with the sticks, you will discover that you will be required to play with the brushes at some time or other, depending on your preferred drumming style and choices. In short, you should be able to play the same things with the brushes as you do with the drumsticks. But for now, let's just cover some of the most basic uses of brushes.

Begin by holding the brush in the center of the snare drum. Then imagine a circle going in an anti-clockwise direction around the drum head. This circle is contained within and occupies the left-side of the drum head. Now imagine that the center, where you now hold the drum brush, is 3 o'clock. The top part of the imagined circle is 12 o'clock, the left side is 9 o'clock and the lower part of the circle is 6 o'clock.

Now run the brush along that imagined circle in an anti-clockwise direction. As you do this, imagine:

3 o'clock as 1
12 o'clock as 2
9 o'clock as 3
and 6 o'clock as beat 4.

So, as you move the brush in this circular motion over the drum head, try to make the brush reach 12 o'clock on the count of 2, 9 o'clock the count of 3, and so on. Slow the brush movement down or speed it up, depending on your timing or count. Try to keep this rhythm going whilst you slightly lift the brush from the head and place it down again on the count of 1 or 3 o'clock. This will accent the first beat and will give a more rhythmic feel. Practice this slowly. When you have practiced this for a while, accent beats 1, 2, 3, and 4.

This is how it looks written down as in exercise 1.

Time Space and Drums   Gravity: Volume Two

Exercise 1

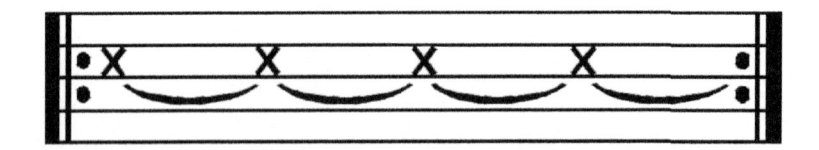

Exercise 2

Now add the RH playing the swing beat rhythm. Notice that there are no signs of these being triplets but they are to be played as triplets even though the second triplet on beats 2 and 4 are missing and no 1/8th note rest is included.

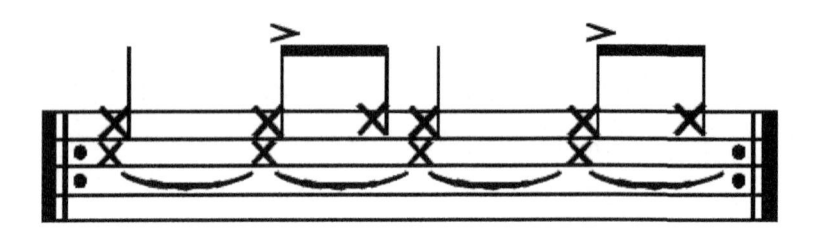

Exercise 3

Now add the LF HH on beats 2 and 4.

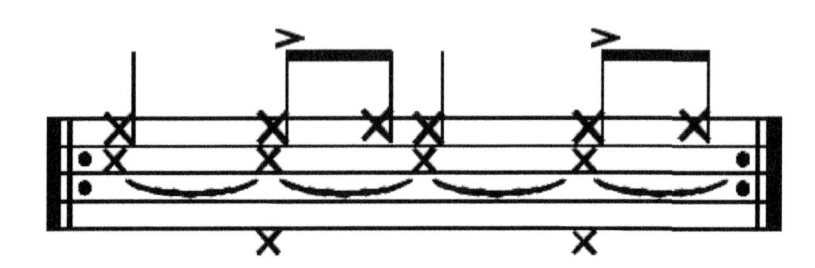

Exercise 4

And finally, add the BD on beats 1 and 3.

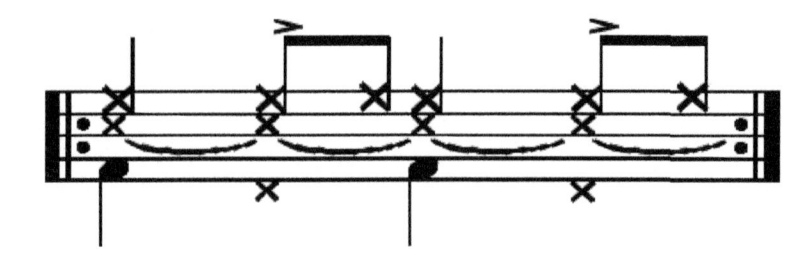

Stephen Hawkins

Exercise 5

You can also do a few tricks with the brushes to create different effects. Hold the brush flat on the head and turn your hand slightly so that when you move your fingers, you get a shimmering sound as the brush moves briskly across the drum head.

Exercise 6

You can also get a good effect by inserting the brush through the cymbal edge and playing it with your fingers. You get a cymbal roll sound.

Exercise 7

You can also get a good effect striking the rim of the SD and adjusting the hand so that you get a fluttering sound on the drum head.

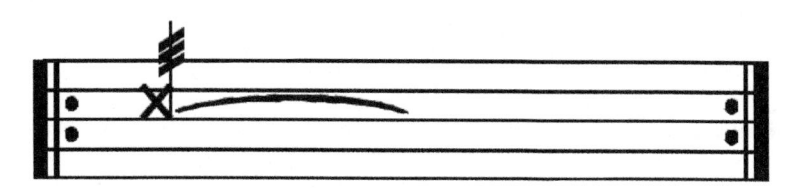

You can incorporate these effects to come up with some interesting rhythms.

Exercise 8 is not written.

Lesson 5

1/16th Note Shuffle Beat.

This next collection of exercises can be a little tricky. This is the 1/16th noted shuffle beat. It sounds like the normal 4/4 shuffle beat pattern with the right-hand played on the Ride Cymbal or HH cymbals but it is doubled up to make 8 shuffles in the bar instead of 4.

But, as you can clearly see, the bass and snare drum still convey the 4/4 pulse. Take a look at it to see what I mean. This rhythm is used on a particular song to great effect. That song is Rosanna, by a band called TOTO.

When I suggested that it could be tricky, I mean that the count can be sometimes tricky. Have a go anyway. But remember, as I mentioned in the previous lesson, the 1/8th and 1/16th notes here sound like triplets and the whole rhythm has a triplet feel to it.

Exercise 1

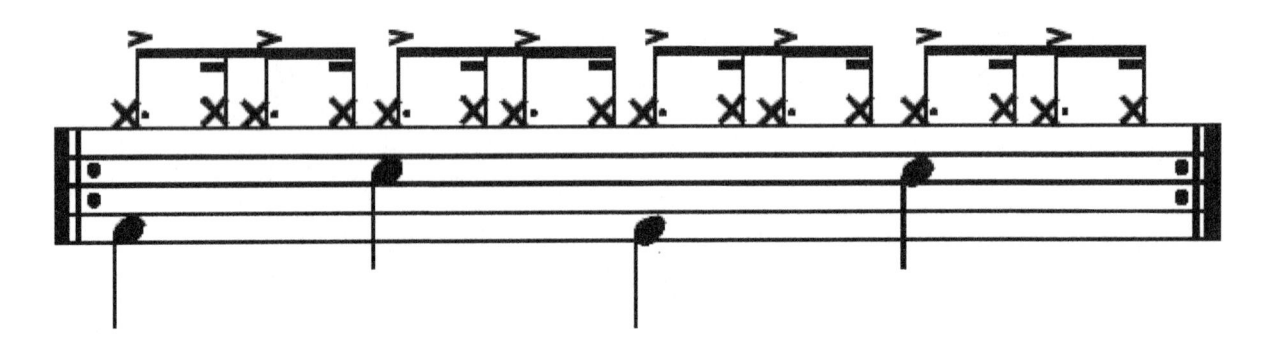

Exercise 2

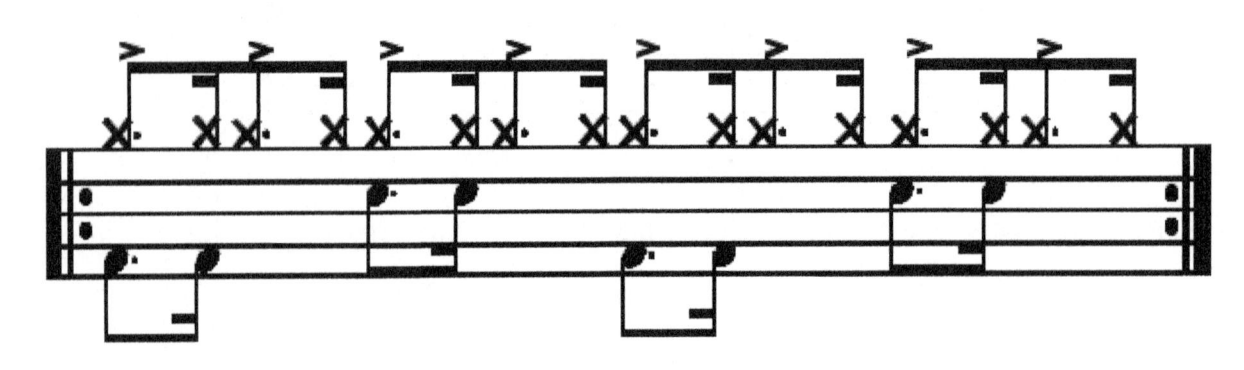

Exercise 3

This time let's just play the RH pattern and the new LH pattern on the snare drum. The left-hand plays ghost notes on the snare drum but is accented on the second and fourth beats. Ghost notes are as the name implies. You can hardly hear them; they are much quieter than the normal and accented notes. This rhythm will demonstrate the importance of dynamics and will give you grounding skills in that area.

Exercise 4

Now try this bass drum pattern. If you have any problems, I would suggest listening to the demonstration audio. You could also purchase any TOTO albums with the tune *Rosanna* on it.

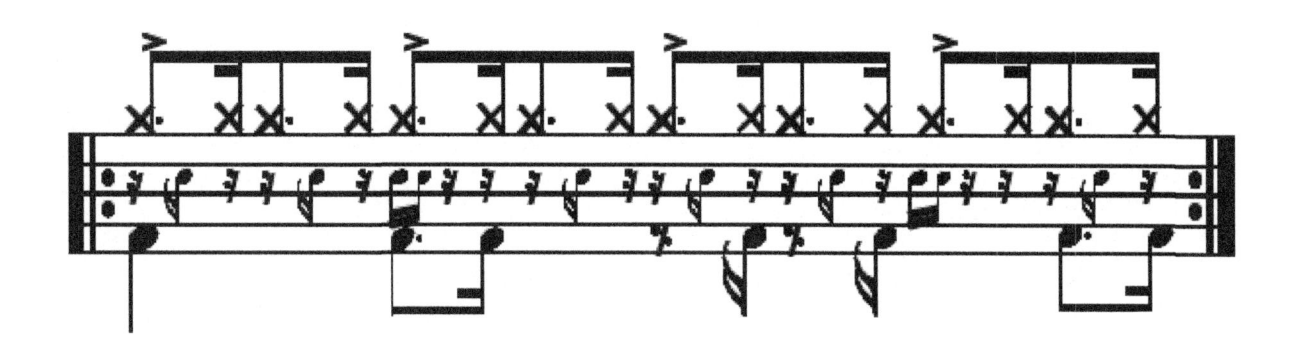

Exercise 5

Now for an exercise that you should study and learn then make a daily part of your practice sessions. This is a bass drum development exercise. It consists of 1 bar of 1/8th notes, a second bar of 1/8th note triplets, and a third bar of 1/16th notes. Play it at the same tempo throughout. You will gain a lot more control over your bass drum using this exercise.

Time Space and Drums Gravity: Volume Two

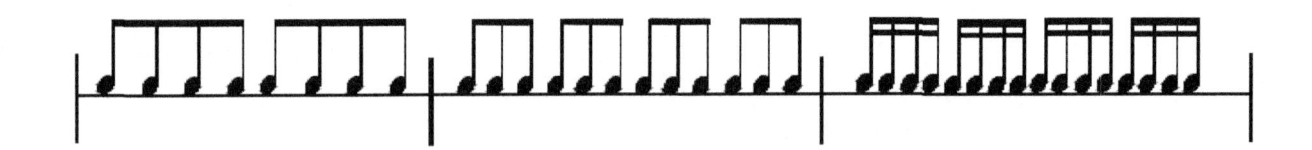

Exercise 6

This time add the LF and HH on beats 1, 2, 3, and 4.

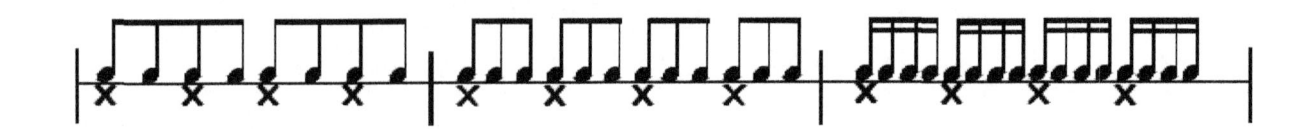

Lesson 6

1/16th Drum Fills

This section deals with a few different drum fills that can be used with the rhythms described in book 1. They are variations on the 4 x 1/16th notes per quarter note. And of course, there are 4 per bar. The sticking for the first exercise is RLR, RLR, etc. These are the first three 1/16th notes in a group of 4 but because the last note is a 1/8th note, there is no need for a 1/16th note rest.

Exercise 1

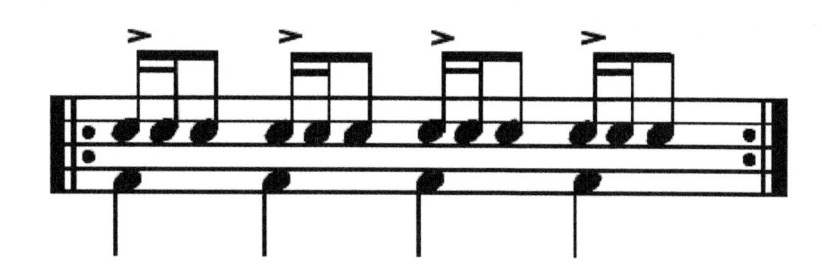

Exercise 2

Now try playing the fill around the toms.

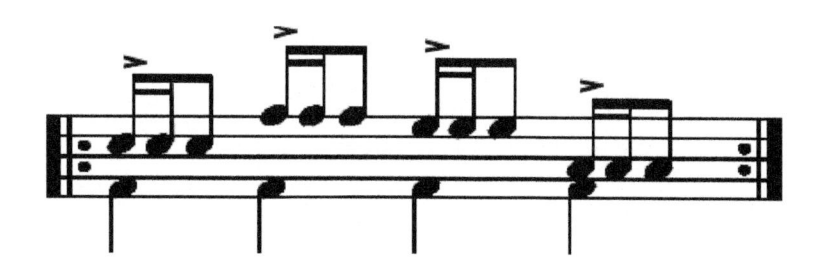

Exercise 3

The sticking for this next exercise is RRL. You will notice that the second 1/16th note played with the LH, is missing. You will also notice that the RH plays 1/8th notes throughout the exercise.

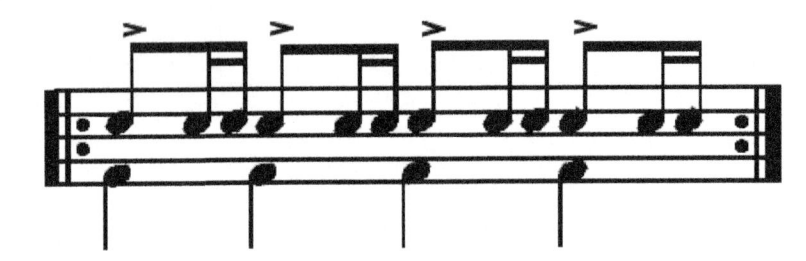

Exercise 4
Again, play the exercise around the toms.

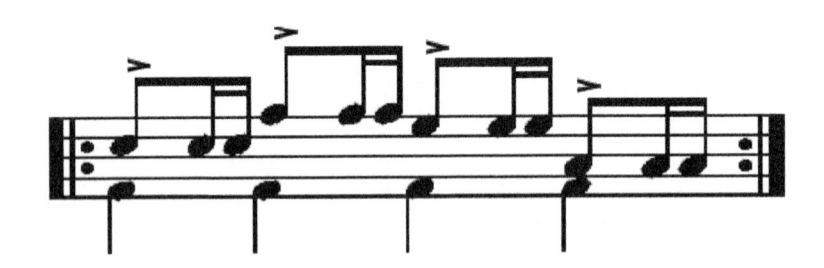

Exercise 5
This time the third 1/16th note from a group of 4 is missing. The sticking is RL L, RL L, etc.

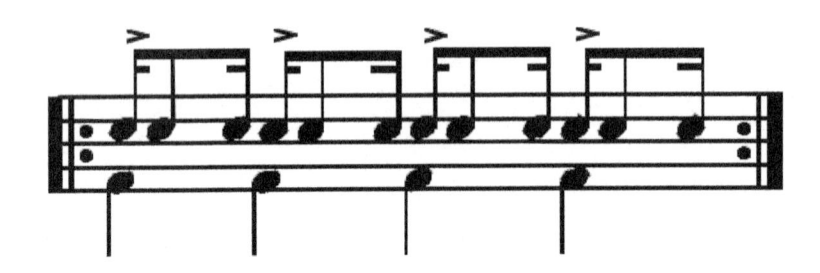

Exercise 6
And again, around the toms.

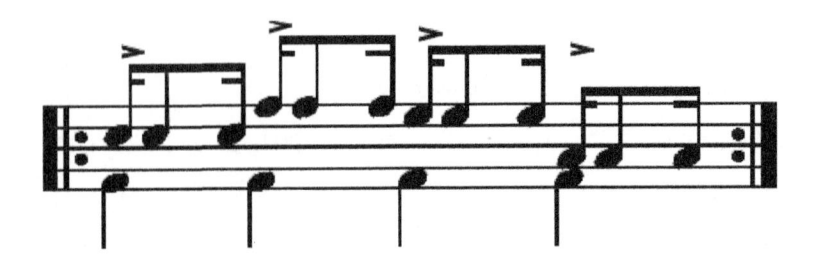

Exercise 7

Now try this mixed variation, based on the fills covered so far.

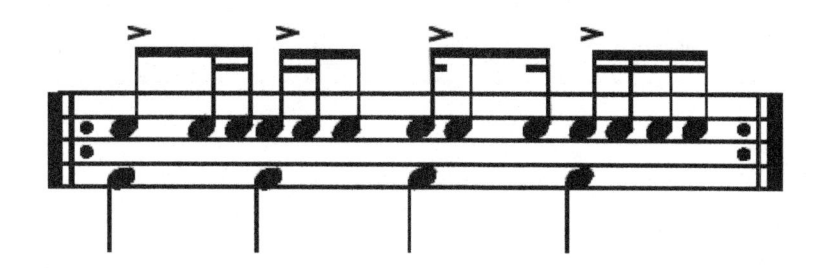

Exercise 8

And again, try playing the fill around the toms.

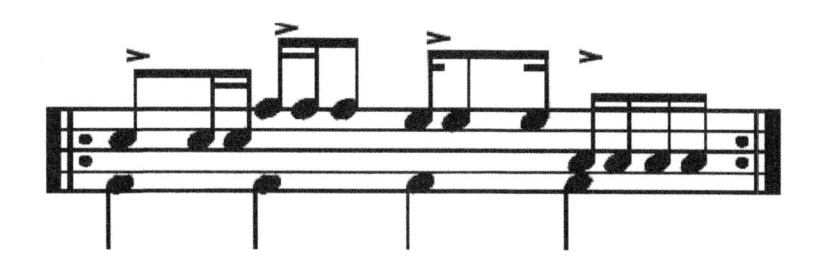

Practice the previous drum fills with a variation of the rhythms covered in book 1. You can even try to create your own fills. Remember to use a manuscript book to invent your own fills to keep a record of your efforts.

Exercise 9

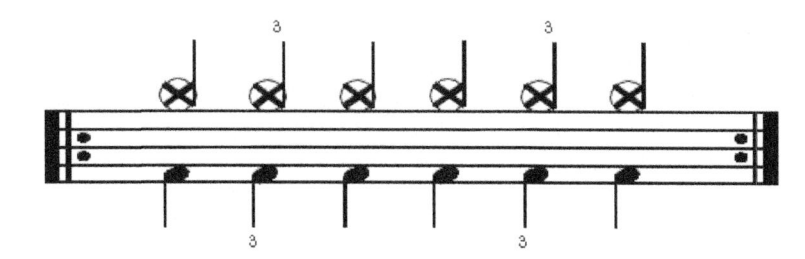

This is a commonly used phrase in drumming and should be practiced playing the rhythms as described in book 1, and the rhythms described here in book 2. Or rock and jazz style rhythms, as illustrated in exercises 10 and 11 next.

Exercise 10

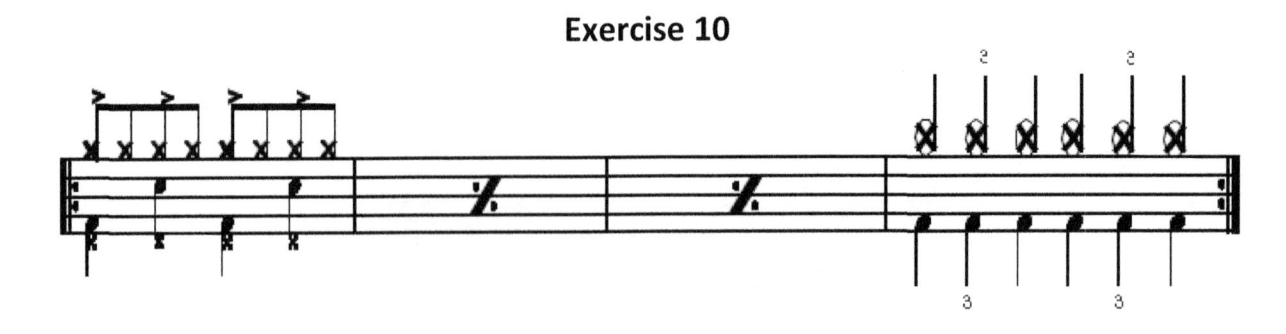

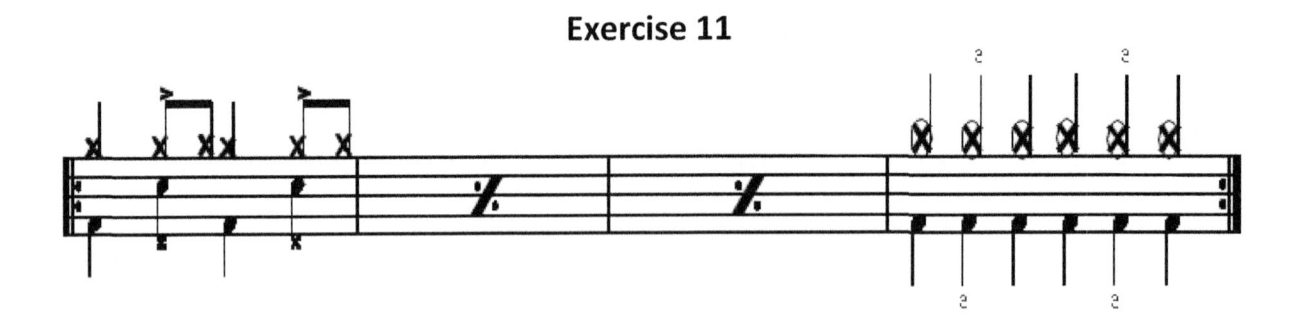

Exercise 11

Time Space and Drums   Gravity: Volume Two

RUDIMENTARY

Triplets

Triplets are not strictly rudiments but for our purposes here, we will treat them as such.

Much like 1/8th notes are doubled to make 1/16th notes and 1/16th notes are doubled (in the amount per bar) to create 32nd notes, so too are triplets. But instead of groups of 2 as in 1.8th notes and groups of 4 as in 1/16th notes, we will be grouping into 3 notes.

So, it can be deduced that you have 1/8th note triplets as well as 1/16th note triplets.

This time, however, there are 12 x 1/8th note triplets in a bar of 4/4 music (3 per quarter note or click of the metronome). And, there are 24 x 1/16th note triplets in a bar of 4/4. For now, though, let's just concentrate on the 1/8th note triplets and as mentioned before, there are 12 1/8th note triplets in a bar of 4/4. See Note Values on page 2.

The above information is covered also on pages 6 and 7 but you don't need to read that section just yet. For now, simply understand that there are 12 x 1/8th note triplets in a bar (3 per quarter note).

The triplet rudiment is really still single strokes R then L then R then L and so on but because there are just 3 notes per quarter note instead of the usual 4, the sticking pattern alters. It now becomes R L R, L R L, then again R L R, L R L. And those are the twelve triplets in a bar of 4/4 music.

The whole thing looks like this:

R L R, L R L, R L R, L R L.

If you count along or play along with the metronome you would be counting:

1   2   3   4
R L R, L R L, **R L R**, L R L.

To hear how this sounds, just speak aloud: One Trip-Let, Two Trip-Let, Three Trip-Let, Four Trip-Let.

In order to understand the continuing flow of this rudiment once you get the basic

Stephen Hawkins

sticking pattern, you should begin to think in groups of 4 instead of groups of 3. Like this:

1   2   3   4
R L R, **L** R L, **R** L R, **L** R L.

In the above example, you would be thinking R... L... R... L... and so on. This is a sort of rocking movement from right to left. And so, it's a good idea to play the first of each group of 3 triplets on the high tom-tom so your hands get used to the packing type pattern. Although, it is important to note that this is just to get you started playing triplets.

You could just simply accent those four quarter notes like this:

\>   \>   \>   \>
R L R, **L** R L, **R** L R, **L** R L.

In the above example, the symbol > means that you play the notes that are below it louder than the other notes.

If you are still a little unsure, reread this rudimentary section several times over until you fully understand and have internalized the notation or mathematically based theory.

Disciplined Experimentation

Once you have the basic feel and flow of the triplet pattern, instead of accenting the first note within each group of 3 triplets, try playing them on different drums randomly and try to keep the constant flow of triplets going continuously.

Just so long as you understand the basic theory and can play the triplets, it will begin to improve over time but try not to get too carried away; instead, be self-disciplined enough to return to the lessons within this book.

Finally, understand that just like part 1 of this series was centered around the single stroke roll, this second book in the series is centered around the triplet rudiment which is really a single stroke toll. However, the triplet groupings make this rudiment more of a feeling or interpretation of the quarter note or pulse of the rhythm.

Now you can return to page 4 and begin lesson 1.

Featured Drummer Recommendations

Buddy Rich

I think most modern articles and reviews about the late Buddy Rich would start something like this... What can I say about Buddy Rich? Well, I always knew Buddy Rich as an older guy, someone who I looked up to but was always old enough to be my own father. And I mention this because as I began to formulate my thoughts about what would be helpful to the student drummer, my mind spoke to me...

What did it say? It said "Wisdom comes with age," but I had a need to question that quote as it seemed like a giant non-sequitur, or the words "wisdom comes with age" didn't follow from the roots and the subsequent journey that drummers such as Buddy Rich take. Incidentally, the same thing applies to Dave Weckl also.

Wisdom comes with age is a non-sequitur. If it wasn't, then all older people would live wealthy lives full of everything they desired. But that isn't the case. So based on these fundamental facts, "wisdom starts early" is my new phrase.

Look at Buddy Rich and you will find that he began succeeding in life from a very early age. Buddy Rich performed throughout his whole childhood as a drummer, starting at 18 months old, and appearing on Broadway shows when he was just 4. He toured Australia at the tender age of 6. At one point in his early career, he was said to be the second-highest-paid child star in the world (Jackie Coogan being the highest paid) and was earning approximately $1,000 a week.

Now to me, that seems to be a very wise child.

I suppose the point of this is to instill in the student drummer something that was taken at a young age: wisdom. When my teachers taught me that "wisdom comes with age," I believed them but it wasn't until later in my life that at the same time I was accepting that at the present I wasn't very wise and so needed guidance in everything that I did. I don't want to get deeper into this; suffice to say that you are wise now.

So, make wise decisions and own that great personal power. Be authentic and accepting of who and what you are: a great drummer on a road to becoming much greater.

So, what else can we learn from Buddy Rich? Well, he was probably the best drummer in the world and possibly even today, although personal preference and styles come into that judgment also.

It is then enough to say that Buddy Rich was the greatest drummer who ever lived and was the master Jazz Drummer. And as we are just being introduced to the Jazz Foundations, we should listen to the very best, which includes Buddy Rich as well as Louis Belson and Gene Krupa.

I personally preferred Buddy Rich's style of drumming but that is purely based on the fact that I never really got to watch or listen to a really great video recording of either Louis Belson or Gene Krupa and so they were less transparent to me. Buddy Rich, on the other hand, has many great videos that show him as probably the best drummer who ever lived, but again, that is just my personal preference and opinion.

If you are new to Buddy Rich, then a good place to start listening to him is the Talk of The Town video recorded in 1969. It's not only a great video in its own right but it also demonstrates triplets and swing style beats better than anyone else could ever do.

Apart from the Buddy Rich Orchestra recordings available as well as audio recordings, a really great resource for jazz style beats played with an emphasis on the music rather than on the drumming are Frank Sinatra Albums who Buddy played for on a regular basis. I particularly recommend L. A is my Lady by Frank Sinatra.

In short, to really master jazz style drumming, every drummer should own a large collection of works by the artists I have mentioned here.

Conclusion

The importance of these beginning exercises throughout this second book and the first rock foundation book cannot be stressed enough. They form a whole foundation on which you will begin to build more tricky rhythms and drum fills. Complete mastery is absolutely essential. But of course, mastery takes time, so play them as well as possible until you can remember; play them all almost effortlessly before moving onto the third and four books in the series.

Again, mastery takes time, so be happy to follow the series knowing that you understand what is written and my explanations. The main reason that I excluded videos from this program was to get the students to read and understand the explanations of the theories we have covered so far. This will also get the students to visualize the rhythms and notes in a way that more deeply engrains them in their memory.

I would, at this point, mention that if you have any doubt whatsoever as to the degree of control you have over any of the exercises covered so far, you should go through books 1 and 2 to iron any little nitty-gritty errors you may be making out. That being said, you should enjoy your new skills and don't be afraid to experiment with the drum fills and rhythms to come up with your own ideas, and/or interpretations.

Good Luck

Stephen Hawkins

Closing Note:
The Time Space and Drums series is intended as a complete program from Part 1 to Part 12. It is strongly advised that you follow the program in order of the parts as they integrate and build on each other. The only thing I can now add is to practice each exercise until you have them all mastered. Mastery comes from paying attention to the most basic fundamentals already covered in each of the exercises within this book.

Once you have perfected each exercise you may like to try them left-handed but that may take time depending on your current skill level.

Free Audio Demonstrations
Please don't forget to visit the following URL to download audio demonstrations of every exercise in this book as soon as possible. You will then receive soma additional tips and guidance through the included essence emails.

www.timespaceanddrums.com/tsd-2cd.html

What's Next
Thank you for choosing Time Space and Drums as one of your learning tools. I hope you enjoyed the process. You can explore more of the series in Constellations Volume One, the third book in the series by searching for "**Rock Drumming Development**" at your favorite bookstore.

Share Your Experience

If you have a moment, please review this Jazz Drumming Foundation book at the store where you bought it. Help other drummers and tell them why you enjoyed the book or what could be improved. Thank you!

Thank you again dear reader and I hope we meet again between the pages of another book. Remember, You rock!

Other Books by The Author

Modern Drumming Concepts
Rock Drumming Foundation Series part. (Six in-depth Drum Lessons).
Jazz Drumming Foundation Series part. (Six in-depth Drum Lessons).
Rock Drumming Development Series part. (Six in-depth Drum Lessons).
Jazz Drumming Development Series part. (Six in-depth Drum Lessons).
Odd Time Drumming Foundation Series part. (Six in-depth Drum Lessons).
Accents and Phrasing Series part. (Four in-depth Drum Lessons).
Basic Latin Drumming Foundation Series part. (Four in-depth Drum Lessons).

The DRUM COACH

Have you ever thought about what it would feel like to make a living as a pro drummer?

If so, then visit the Drum Coach website. I might be for YOU!

The purpose of the Drum Coach blog is not only to provide drummers with valuable information but also to help them share their passions.

The Drum Coach provides all types of drumming information from beginner lessons right up to professional level playing skills, as well as personal self*(drummer)*-improvement essentials – there's something here no matter your skill level!

Some of the most important information on this website comes from my personal experiences as a percussionist and musician for over 35 years. So, I invite you to take advantage of the Drum Coach Experience, whose aim is to provide high-quality, on-demand information for drummers as they travel along their journey to achieve their personal drumming goals and ambitions.

Our commitment to our readers is always 100%! If you have any problems, questions, or concerns, just let us know and we'll help you take care of the situation as quickly as possible.

And remember to **Stay In Time!** and continue to **Rock!**

DRUM COACH TIPS
Visit thedrumcoach.com to get weekly Drum Coach Action Tips

Printed in Great Britain
by Amazon